King Sejong's Gift

Seong min Yoo

Text copyright © 2025
Illustration copyright © 2025

All rights reserved. No part of this publication may be reproduced or transmitted in any form or by any means, electronic or mechanical, including photocopying, recording or by any information storage and retrieval system now known or to be invented, without permission in writing from the publisher.

Layout and design by Seong min Yoo
ISBN 978-1-0693151-9-9

Able Beaver Press Co. fuels creativity and continues to publish books for every reader. Thank you for buying an authorized edition of this book. The artwork in this book was rendered in watercolour and gouache.

Written and illustrated by Seong min Yoo
Proofing by Scott MacKenzie

2 4 6 8 10 9 7 5 3

For all those who find joy in every new word

Emily likes Korean music. She enjoys the melody but not so much the lyrics. Mom asks one day, "Emily, do you know what those songs are about?" "No, but they would be more enjoyable if I understand them." Emily answers.

"Can you guess by any chance who made the Korean alphabet?" Mom asks. "Well, Hmmm, I'm not sure." She replies. "It was created by King Sejong the Great of the Joseon Dynasty in 1443." Mom says. "Oh, I see!" Emily exclaims.

"The literacy rate was not very high at that time among commoners as the written Chinese characters were used only by the upper class. It was a different form to the spoken language and was restricted as it was so difficult for ordinary citizens to learn. So they were having trouble expressing their thoughts or communicating on a daily basis."

Mom continues. "King Sejong, who loved his people and felt sorry for the struggles that they had faced, wanted to help them get the proper education they deserved." "Oh, so what happened to them?" Emily asks.

"King Sejong published Hunminjeongeum which is the original name of the Korean alphabet, it means the right sounds to teach the people, and it explained the logic and science behind it.

ㄱㄴㄷㄹㅁㅂㅅ
ㅇㅈㅊㅋㅌㅍㅎ
ㅏㅑㅓㅕㅗㅛㅜ
ㅠㅡㅣ

It is remarkably easy to learn, with its own unique sounds, separate from Chinese characters, consisting of 28 letters of 17 consonants and 11 vowels, but 4 gradually disappeared, leading to the current 24 letters." She explains.

"Later on in 1912, the name of Hangeul was coined by Korean linguist Ju Si-gyeong. Han means great and geul means script." Mom cites.

"Hangeul is one of the most logically designed phonetic alphabets in the world creating more than 11,000 different syllable blocks." Mom says. "Oh, wow, that is beyond my imagination." Emily is amazed. "Yes, it is, isn't it?" Mom smiles. "I wonder what Hangeul looks like and how it is written." Emily is curious.

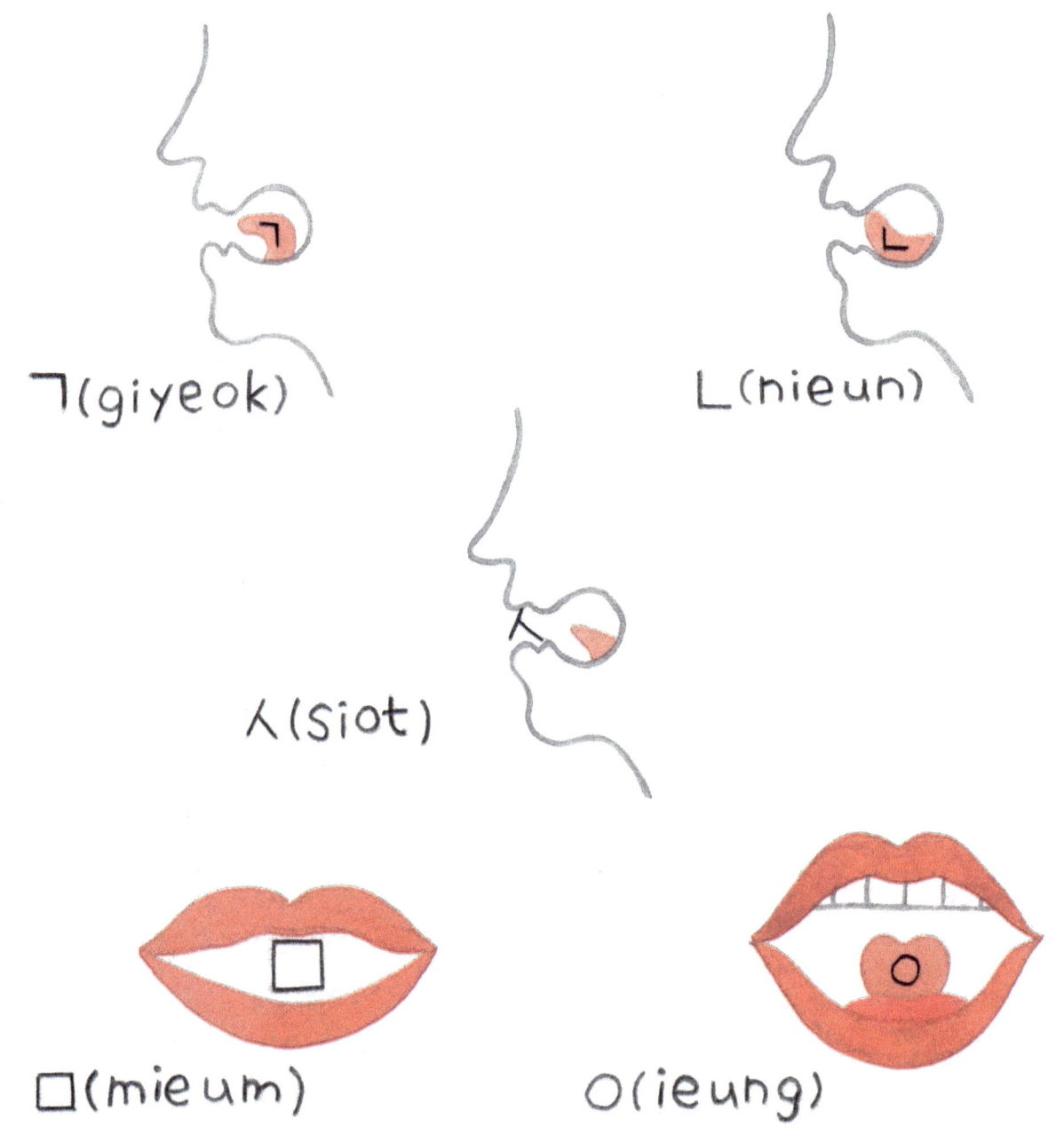

"Here they are, the five basic consonants are ㄱ(g) ㄴ(n) ㅁ(m) ㅅ(s) ㅇ(ng)" Mom points out. "These are so fascinating." Emily shouts with joy. Mom mentions that Korean consonants are a sound that comes from the back of the tongue or throat like ㄱ ㅇ, a sound made using the front part of the tongue like ㄴ ㅅ and a sound of two lips touching like ㅁ.

Emily tries to imitate the sound. She pronounces giyeok triumphantly. "Yes, you are really good." Mom says. She tells Emily that more letters can be created by adding strokes of one or two to the basic consonants. ㅋ-k(kieuk) ㄷ-d(digeut) ㅌ-t(tieut) ㄹ-r(rieul) ㅂ-b(bieup) ㅍ-p(pieup) ㅈ-j(jieut) ㅊ-ch(chieut) ㅎ-h(hieut)

Sky

Person

Earth

Basic Vowels

"Hangeul is very fun to learn. What about vowels, how are they made and how do they look?" Emily couldn't wait to discover more. "The basic vowels were made out of three elements and they were derived from the shapes representing heaven, earth and human. • represented the roundness of the sky, — represented the flat earth and | symbolized a person who was standing between the sky and the earth."

"Oh, what did they sound like then?" Emily asks. "The sky symbol represented a sound similar to Ah, the earth was similar to Eu, the person was similar to Ee. King Sejong applied this oriental philosophy to embody the harmonization between all 3 elements, developing more vowels." Mom says.

"And these three basic shapes were combined to create the first six vowels, ㅏ (ah), ㅓ (eo), ㅗ(o), ㅜ(oo), ㅡ(eu), ㅣ (ee), and double vowels were created by adding another horizontal or vertical stroke, ㅑ (ya), ㅕ (yeo), ㅘ(wah), ㅛ(yo), ㅞ(weh), ㅠ (yu)." Mom says.

"It is really impressive how these letters were created based on the universe." Emily says with admiration. Mom tells Emily that Hangeul was first officially adopted in 1894 with widespread effects to promote its goodness, however there were incidents that prohibited the use of the Korean language, such as during the Japanese colonial period.

Mom goes on. "Then with the end of the occupation in 1945, Korean was re-established as the official language and so we are able to use the wonderful Hangeul today."

"Korean people also celebrate Hangeul day." Mom says. "Oh, really?" Emily is surprised with the fact. "It's annually on October 9th to show appreciation for King Sejong's creativity and honouring the excellence of Hangeul, it was registered with UNESCO in 1997 as well. Its inclusion recognizes Hangeul as a scientific and important piece of cultural heritage." Mom states.

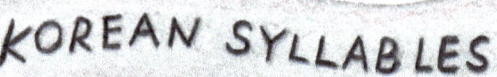

KOREAN SYLLABLES

| CONSO-NANT | VOWEL |

ㄱ ㅏ = 가

| CONSO-NANT 1 | VOWEL |
| CONSONANT 2 | |

ㄱ ㅏ = 강
ㅇ

"That is wonderful!" Emily cheers proudly. Mom shows her the basic shape of syllables in Korean which are consonant+vowel, for example '가'(ga) or consonant+vowel+consonant, like the word 강(gang). She lets Emily know Korean letters are written like building a house.

"I think I can write Hangeul now." Emily announces confidently. "H pronounces ㅎ, a pronounces ㅏ and n pronounces ㄴ." Emily accomplishes the first letter and concentrates for the second one. "And g pronounces ㄱ, eu pronounces ㅡ and l pronounces ㄹ."

She completes it slowly but clearly 한글. The horizontal, vertical and circle are all harmonized magically. She is delighted. "That is so neat." Mom lovingly embraces her. Now Emily knows more about Korean song lyrics. She cherishes Korean music even more as she recalls the joy of learning Korean.

Emily already imagines asking for directions and ordering food in Korean. She would love to learn about other captivating Korean traditions too. Knowing and understanding new words make her feel different. She really looks forward to the day she can speak this beautiful language freely. It will lead to many adventures.

Her passion extends to various art forms. She especially loves all the simple and pure images of nature and has been writing and illustrating children's book for more than 10 years. She was born in Korea and moved to Canada in 2001 and lives with her husband and daughter in Toronto.

More books by Seong min Yoo

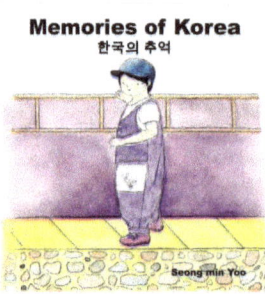
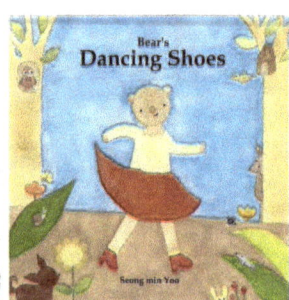

www.ingramcontent.com/pod-product-compliance
Lightning Source LLC
Chambersburg PA
CBHW061151070526
44584CB00034B/4483